# HAIL to the CHIEF

★ ★ ★ ★ ★

## The American Presidency

Don Robb ★ Illustrated by Alan Witschonke

ini Charlesbridge

*To Jack, from Poppy.*
*You're already my choice for president.*
— D. R.

*To Serge and Darrell, who took a leap of faith.*
*I hope they feel that it was worth it.*
— A. W.

★    ★    ★    ★    ★

Text copyright © 2010 by Don Robb
Illustrations copyright © 2000 by Alan Witschonke
All rights reserved, including the right of reproduction in whole or in part in any form.
Charlesbridge and colophon are registered trademarks of Charlesbridge Publishing, Inc.

Published by Charlesbridge
85 Main Street
Watertown, MA 02472
(617) 926-0329
www.charlesbridge.com

Printed in China
(hc) 10 9 8 7 6 5 4 3 2 1
(sc) 10 9 8 7 6 5 4 3 2 1

**Library of Congress Cataloging-in-Publication Data**
Hail to the chief : the American presidency / Don Robb ; illustrated by Alan Witschonke.
p. cm.
Originally published: 2000.
Summary: Primary text describes the powers and duties of the presidency while subtext highlights the accomplishments of individual presidents. Includes a timeline.
ISBN 978-1-58089-285-8 (reinforced for library use)
ISBN 978-1-58089-286-5 (softcover)
1. Presidents—United States—Juvenile literature.  I. Witschonke, Alan, 1953– ill.
II. Title.
JK517.R63 2010
973.09'9—dc22
2009044117

Illustrations done in colored inks on Fabriano watercolor paper
Display type and text type set in Stuyvesant and Cochin
Printed and bound February 2010 by Jade Productions in Heyuan, Guangdong, China
Production supervision by Brian G. Walker
Designed by Diane M. Earley

★    ★    ★    ★    ★

**Acknowledgments**
Special thanks to David Montgomery for his comments on the text and illustrations. Thanks also to the following organizations and individuals for granting permission to use photographs as references for some of the illustrations in this book:
p. 5 (right): illustration based on original photo by Neil Johnson from *The Battle of Lexington and Concord*,
published by Four Winds Press/Macmillan Publishing Co./Simon & Schuster Inc. © 1992 by Neil Johnson.
Reprinted with permission of Neil Johnson, c/o Mary Jack Wald Associates, Inc. 111 East 14th Street, New York, New York 10003;
p. 9 (top left): illustration inspired by "Crossville, Tennessee, October 1935" by Ben Shahn;
p. 11 (top): original photograph © U.S. Army; p. 23 (top): original photograph © Bettmann/CORBIS;
p. 27 (left): original photograph © George Mobley/NGS Image Collection

# PRESIDENTIAL POWERS

Every four years we elect a president to lead our country. Because the United States is such a powerful nation, our president is one of the most important leaders in the world.

The Constitution, our basic set of rules, lists many duties of the president. As our country has grown, so has the job of our president.

The president takes an oath to "preserve and protect" the Constitution. He is the "executive power" of the country, which means that he leads our federal government and enforces our laws.

Under the Constitution the president is commander in chief of all our armed forces.

The president can recommend laws for Congress to consider. Every January he reports to Congress in his "State of the Union" speech.

With Senate approval the president appoints members of the Supreme Court and other important government officials.

He can ask heads of government departments (his cabinet) for their opinions and advice.

The president receives foreign ambassadors and, with Senate approval, appoints our ambassadors to other countries.

He makes and signs treaties, though the Senate must agree to them.

When *George Washington,* hero of the Revolutionary War, became our first president, he was the only president anywhere in the world. Other countries had kings, queens, and emperors who had inherited their thrones. Only in America did the people take part in electing a president to lead them.

Some people wanted to call him "Your Majesty," but Washington insisted he was just "Mr. President," no different from his fellow citizens.

As the first president, Washington helped lay the foundation of our government. He became an example for all the presidents who followed him.

Because he refused to run for a third term, no president except **Franklin Roosevelt** has served more than two terms. (Now the Constitution limits the president to two terms.)

Washington appointed all the members of the first Supreme Court.

He named the first heads of government departments. In his day, these were the secretaries of state, treasury, and war, and the attorney general.

These officials became known as the president's cabinet, even though the Constitution never mentions this word. Today there are fifteen departments in the cabinet.

# LEADERS IN WAR

Many Americans honor *Abraham Lincoln* as our greatest president. Tall and lean, he was born in a frontier log cabin. He became a successful lawyer, a popular public speaker, and a member of Congress.

As commander in chief, this kind, gentle, and wise leader held the Union together during the terrible years of the Civil War and brought an end to slavery.

In the War of 1812 **James Madison** governed the country from Virginia after the British army burned Washington.

**James Polk** led the country in a war against Mexico in 1846.

**William McKinley** prayed for divine guidance before asking Congress to declare war on Spain in 1898.

Harry Truman sent American forces to fight communism in Korea, as **John Kennedy**, **Lyndon Johnson**, and **Richard Nixon** did in Vietnam.

In 1990 **George H. W. Bush** ordered U.S. troops to the Persian Gulf when Iraq invaded Kuwait.

Under **Bill Clinton**, American forces took part in an international effort to bring peace to Kosovo.

**George W. Bush** sent American troops to fight global terrorism in Afghanistan and Iraq.

Three of our presidents, **Zachary Taylor**, **Ulysses Grant**, and **Dwight Eisenhower**, were elected largely because of their reputations as wartime generals.

# LEADERS IN HARD TIMES

Another of our greatest presidents, *Franklin Roosevelt,* led the nation through difficult times.

In the Great Depression members of one out of every three American families lost their jobs. Millions of men, women, and children faced poverty and hunger. By asking Congress to pass laws easing the effects of the hard times, Roosevelt gave hope to our struggling country.

Until the Great Depression of 1929, economic hard times were called "panics."

★

The panic of 1837 lasted until 1843 and cost **Martin Van Buren** any chance of reelection.

★

In the past, government did not do much to manage the economy, so people were not surprised that **James Buchanan** did nothing to help poor farmers during the panic of 1857.

★

**Ulysses Grant** (in 1873) and **Grover Cleveland** (in 1893) both asked Congress to build up gold reserves to restore faith in America's currency.

By 1930 the Great Depression had become so severe that **Herbert Hoover** began limited aid to businesses, home owners, and farmers.

★

In 2009 **Barack Obama** proposed government action to help struggling banks, businesses, and home owners.

★

**Harry Truman**, **John Kennedy**, **Richard Nixon**, **Gerald Ford**, **Jimmy Carter**, and **George H. W. Bush** all proposed actions such as price controls, tax cuts, and spending programs to help ease recessions.

# ENFORCING THE LAWS

When *Dwight Eisenhower* was president, the Supreme Court ruled that segregation—separating people by skin color—was illegal in America's schools. How could he make sure that the Court's ruling, now the law of the land, was obeyed?

Eisenhower had led American forces during World War II, which taught him the importance of taking difficult but necessary actions. To end segregation he ordered federal troops to make sure that all children could attend school safely.

Presidents sometimes take action to enforce unpopular laws.

**George Washington** sent troops to Pennsylvania to put down a revolt by farmers protesting high taxes.

To protect the right of every citizen to vote, **Lyndon Johnson** sent federal observers to elections in several states.

On at least one occasion a president refused to uphold the law. **Andrew Jackson** ordered the Creek, Chickasaw, Choctaw, Cherokee, and Seminole nations to move to reservations in the West. The Supreme Court ruled that his order was unconstitutional, but Jackson sent in the army, and the Native Americans were forced off their lands.

When France offered to sell Louisiana to the United States, *Thomas Jefferson* had a decision to make. The Constitution did not say whether he could—or could not—buy land.

Jefferson decided that he could. So in 1803 the Louisiana Purchase more than doubled the size of the United States—all for less than three cents an acre!

In 1819 **James Monroe** bought Florida from Spain.

★

**Franklin Pierce** bought a strip of land from Mexico in 1853 so that a railroad could be built across it. That land became part of New Mexico and Arizona.

When **Andrew Johnson**'s secretary of state, William Seward, proposed buying a vast area in the far north, people were astonished. Why would anyone want "Seward's Folly"? Since then people have found gold and oil there—and Alaska is our forty-ninth state!

# THE PRESIDENTS AND CONGRESS

Under the Constitution presidents may propose new laws to Congress. After the assassination of John Kennedy, *Lyndon Johnson* convinced Congress to pass more than a dozen laws that he and the fallen president had wanted.

Some of these laws protected consumers or guaranteed equal rights in jobs, housing, and voting. Others set standards for clean air and water. Still others created programs for children and provided medical care to the poor and elderly.

**Franklin Roosevelt** made government a part of everyday life when he created Social Security—government payments to retired people—and started providing money and other help to poor families and people without jobs.

★

**Woodrow Wilson** and **Theodore Roosevelt** led Congress to strengthen laws regulating business.

Congress responded to **Harry Truman** by providing money for foreign aid, raising the minimum wage, and getting rid of slums.

★

Presidents **Ronald Reagan** and **George H. W. Bush** worked to reduce the role of government. Under **Bill Clinton** the budget was balanced for the first time since the 1960s.

# LEADERS IN THE WORLD

When World War I broke out in Europe, *Woodrow Wilson* tried hard to keep our country neutral. When American ships were attacked and American citizens died in battles at sea, the country was forced to enter the war.

When it was over, Wilson met with the leaders of Britain, France, and Italy. He suggested bringing the countries of the world together as the League of Nations, to end war forever. Unfortunately the peace lasted for only twenty years.

President **George Washington** had warned against "entangling alliances," but since his time the United States has grown so powerful that our country cannot avoid close ties with other nations.

★

The U.S. has always been interested in Latin America. **James Monroe** warned Europe to keep "hands off," **William Howard Taft** advanced American business interests in the region, and **Franklin Roosevelt** promised to make the U.S. a good neighbor to Latin American countries.

In the 1850s **Millard Fillmore** opened relations with Japan.

★

In the 1970s **Richard Nixon** improved a difficult relationship with China. Later **Jimmy Carter** and **Bill Clinton** brought together leaders of the Middle East in a search for peace.

★

**Ronald Reagan**'s policies helped to end America's long cold war with the Soviet Union (Russia).

# LEADERS OF THEIR PARTIES

By the time *Andrew Jackson* was elected, political parties were becoming important. Since his day, the president has always been the leader of his party, though the Constitution says nothing at all about political parties.

Jackson used his party, the Democrats, to run his election campaign. His followers called him "a man of the people." He rewarded them with government jobs. This power to appoint officials gives presidents great influence over the party.

Political parties first played a role in the election of 1800. The Federalists, led by **John Adams**, favored a strong central government. **Thomas Jefferson**'s Democratic-Republicans argued that the states should have more power.

★

Today political parties are a major part of the election process, and presidents still use their power of appointment to reward supporters and build party loyalty.

The cost of campaigns has now become so great that presidents must spend much of their time raising money for their party. This has led to calls for spending limits.

★

**Ronald Reagan**, the "Great Communicator," had a gift for attracting huge crowds and large donations at party rallies.

# DARK-HORSE CANDIDATES

Political parties nominate a candidate to run for president. Usually they choose the best-known party member. In 1844, though, the Democrats had a problem.

Four different candidates all had support, but none had enough to be nominated. Finally the party chose *James Polk*. He was the first "dark horse"—an unknown who beats out famous candidates and wins the nomination.

Before primary elections became common, party leaders often made deals at conventions. Sometimes the leaders chose a compromise candidate.

**Franklin Pierce, Rutherford Hayes, James Garfield**, and **Benjamin Harrison** all defeated better-known men for nomination.

Dark-horse candidate **Warren Harding** was chosen by a handful of Republican leaders late one night in 1920.

Because dark-horse candidates usually have limited support, none of these presidents rank among the country's stronger leaders.

In 1948 everyone thought that *Harry Truman* could not win a second term in office. Everyone, that is, except Truman himself. Starting with a rousing speech to the convention, he surprised his party and the nation.

Truman toured the country by train, stopping to give more than three hundred speeches. Some newspapers predicted that his opponent would win, but the voters went for Truman.

Instead of traveling the country, in 1888 **Benjamin Harrison** made reporters and political leaders come to him.

**William McKinley** ran a similar "front porch" campaign from his home in 1896, as did **Warren Harding** in 1920. It worked: They were all elected.

In the disputed presidential election of 2000, the Supreme Court had to settle the issue and ruled in favor of **George W. Bush**.

Slogans help win elections. In 1840 the slogan "Tippecanoe and Tyler, Too!" helped elect **William Henry Harrison**, hero of the Battle of Tippecanoe, and his running mate, **John Tyler**.

One of the simplest yet most effective slogans helped to elect **Dwight Eisenhower** in 1952 and 1956: "I Like Ike."

**Grover Cleveland** has the distinction of being the only man to win the presidency (in 1884), then lose it (in 1888), then win it again (in 1892).

# REMOVING A PRESIDENT

Congress and President *Andrew Johnson* disagreed on how to restore the Union after the Civil War and on how the defeated South should be treated. Their argument became so bitter that the House of Representatives impeached Johnson. They accused him of disobeying laws that Congress had passed, and asked the Senate to put him on trial.

By a margin of just one vote, the Senate refused to convict him, and Johnson served out the rest of his term.

There are two steps to removing a president from office. The House of Representatives impeaches a president by a majority vote accusing him of "high crimes and misdemeanors." The Senate then holds a trial. The president is removed from office only if two-thirds of the senators vote for conviction.

In Johnson's case the crime was firing a cabinet officer without the approval of Congress.

**Bill Clinton** was impeached in 1998 for lying about his personal life to a grand jury, but the Senate acquitted him.

In 1974 the House Judiciary Committee voted to recommend the impeachment of **Richard Nixon** for blocking an investigation into crimes committed during the 1972 election. Before the full House could act, however, Nixon resigned from office.

In 1841, for the first time, a president died in office. The Constitution was clear: The duties of the office now went to the vice president. But was the vice president, *John Tyler*, now "president" by title, or was he just an "acting president"?

Tyler was certain that he deserved to be called president. He even refused to open mail addressed to "the acting president." Ever since, when a president has died in office, the vice president has taken the title of president.

Nine times in our history the vice president has assumed the office of president.

★

Presidential assassinations brought to office **Andrew Johnson** in 1865, **Chester Arthur** in 1881, **Theodore Roosevelt** in 1901, and **Lyndon Johnson** in 1963.

★

In addition to Tyler three others have succeeded to office on the death of the president: **Millard Fillmore** in 1850, **Calvin Coolidge** in 1923, and **Harry Truman** in 1945.

After finishing the term of a president who died in office, **Theodore Roosevelt**, **Calvin Coolidge**, **Harry Truman**, and **Lyndon Johnson** were later elected to terms of their own.

★

The only president to resign from office was **Richard Nixon**, in 1974. The vice president, **Gerald Ford**, immediately became president.

# PRESIDENTIAL FAMILIES

He was a busy and active president, but *Theodore Roosevelt* still found time to enjoy his family. People have always thought of our president as the head of the "American family."

Roosevelt's six children turned the White House into a lively and hectic family home. They played tag in the hallways, scrambled through the president's office, and rode ponies and played baseball on the lawn. They also kept pets: dogs, rabbits, birds, a badger, and even a black bear cub. The public loved the president, his family, and their pets!

Two bachelors have been elected president. **James Buchanan** never married; **Grover Cleveland** was the only president to be married in the White House. His daughter Esther is the only child ever actually born in the White House itself.

★

By far the largest presidential family was **John Tyler**'s: six daughters and eight sons.

Politics sometimes seems to run in families. **John Quincy Adams** was the son of **John Adams**; **George W. Bush**, the son of **George H. W. Bush**; **Benjamin Harrison**, the grandson of **William Henry Harrison**; and **Franklin Roosevelt**, the cousin of **Theodore Roosevelt**.

★

When **Barack Obama** was elected, another young family moved into the White House.

# PRESIDENTS OF THE UNITED STATES

| PRESIDENT | TERM | PARTY | BORN | ELECTED FROM | DIED |
|---|---|---|---|---|---|
| **George Washington** *(4–5, 10, 16)* | 1789–1798 | Federalist | 1732, Virginia | Virginia | 1799 |
| **John Adams** *(18, 28)* | 1798–1801 | Federalist | 1735, Massachusetts | Massachusetts | 1826 |
| **Thomas Jefferson** *(12–13, 18)* | 1801–1809 | Dem.–Rep. | 1743, Virginia | Virginia | 1826 |
| **James Madison** *(6)* | 1809–1817 | Dem.–Rep. | 1751, Virginia | Virginia | 1836 |
| **James Monroe** *(12, 16)* | 1817–1825 | Dem.–Rep. | 1758, Virginia | Virginia | 1831 |
| **John Quincy Adams** *(28)* | 1825–1829 | Nat.–Rep. | 1767, Massachusetts | Massachusetts | 1848 |
| **Andrew Jackson** *(10, 18–19)* | 1829–1837 | Democrat | 1767, South Carolina | Tennessee | 1845 |
| **Martin Van Buren** *(8)* | 1837–1841 | Democrat | 1782, New York | New York | 1862 |
| **William Henry Harrison** *(22, 28)* | 1841 | Whig | 1773, Virginia | Ohio | 1841 |
| **John Tyler** *(22, 26–27, 28)* | 1841–1845 | Whig | 1790, Virginia | Virginia | 1862 |
| **James K. Polk** *(6, 20–21)* | 1845–1849 | Democrat | 1795, North Carolina | Tennessee | 1849 |
| **Zachary Taylor** *(6)* | 1849–1850 | Whig | 1784, Virginia | Virginia | 1850 |
| **Millard Fillmore** *(16, 26)* | 1850–1853 | Whig | 1800, New York | New York | 1874 |
| **Franklin Pierce** *(12, 20)* | 1853–1857 | Democrat | 1804, New Hampshire | New Hampshire | 1869 |
| **James Buchanan** *(8, 28)* | 1857–1861 | Democrat | 1791, Pennsylvania | Pennsylvania | 1868 |
| **Abraham Lincoln** *(6–7)* | 1861–1865 | Republican | 1809, Kentucky | Illinois | 1865 |
| **Andrew Johnson** *(12, 24–25, 26)* | 1865–1869 | Nat. Union | 1808, North Carolina | Tennessee | 1875 |
| **Ulysses S. Grant** *(6, 8)* | 1869–1877 | Republican | 1822, Ohio | Ohio | 1885 |
| **Rutherford B. Hayes** *(20)* | 1877–1881 | Republican | 1822, Ohio | Ohio | 1893 |
| **James A. Garfield** *(20)* | 1881 | Republican | 1831, Ohio | Ohio | 1881 |
| **Chester A. Arthur** *(26)* | 1881–1885 | Republican | 1830, Vermont | New York | 1886 |

*Numbers in parentheses refer to the pages on which each president appears. Numbers in bold refer to pages on which the president is featured in the main text.*

| President | Term | Party | Born | Elected From | Died |
|---|---|---|---|---|---|
| **Grover Cleveland** *(8, 22, 28)* | 1885–1889 1893–1897 | Democrat | 1837, New Jersey | New York | 1908 |
| **Benjamin Harrison** *(20, 22, 28)* | 1889–1893 | Republican | 1833, Ohio | Indiana | 1901 |
| **William McKinley** *(6, 22)* | 1897–1901 | Republican | 1843, Ohio | Ohio | 1901 |
| **Theodore Roosevelt** *(14, 26, 28–29)* | 1901–1909 | Republican | 1858, New York | New York | 1919 |
| **William H. Taft** *(16)* | 1909–1913 | Republican | 1857, Ohio | Ohio | 1930 |
| **Woodrow Wilson** *(14, 16–17)* | 1913–1921 | Democrat | 1856, Virginia | New Jersey | 1924 |
| **Warren G. Harding** *(20, 22)* | 1921–1923 | Republican | 1865, Ohio | Ohio | 1923 |
| **Calvin Coolidge** *(26)* | 1923–1929 | Republican | 1872, Vermont | Massachusetts | 1933 |
| **Herbert Hoover** *(8)* | 1929–1933 | Republican | 1874, Iowa | California | 1964 |
| **Franklin D. Roosevelt** *(4, 8–9, 14, 16, 28)* | 1933–1945 | Democrat | 1882, New York | New York | 1945 |
| **Harry S. Truman** *(6, 8, 14, 22–23, 26)* | 1945–1953 | Democrat | 1884, Missouri | Missouri | 1972 |
| **Dwight D. Eisenhower** *(6, 10–11, 22)* | 1953–1961 | Republican | 1890, Texas | New York | 1969 |
| **John F. Kennedy** *(6, 8)* | 1961–1963 | Democrat | 1917, Massachusetts | Massachusetts | 1963 |
| **Lyndon B. Johnson** *(6, 10, 14–15, 26)* | 1963–1969 | Democrat | 1908, Texas | Texas | 1973 |
| **Richard M. Nixon** *(6, 8, 16, 24, 26)* | 1969–1974 | Republican | 1913, California | California | 1994 |
| **Gerald R. Ford** *(8, 26)* | 1974–1977 | Republican | 1913, Nebraska | Michigan | 2006 |
| **Jimmy Carter** *(8, 16)* | 1977–1981 | Democrat | 1924, Georgia | Georgia | |
| **Ronald Reagan** *(14, 16, 18)* | 1981–1989 | Republican | 1911, Illinois | California | 2004 |
| **George H. W. Bush** *(6, 8, 14, 28)* | 1989–1993 | Republican | 1924, Massachusetts | Texas | |
| **Bill Clinton** *(6, 14, 16, 24)* | 1993–2001 | Democrat | 1946, Arkansas | Arkansas | |
| **George W. Bush** *(6, 22, 28)* | 2001–2009 | Republican | 1946, Connecticut | Texas | |
| **Barack Obama** *(8, 28)* | 2009– | Democrat | 1961, Hawaii | Illinois | |

*Dem.–Rep. = Democratic Republican; Nat.–Rep. = National Republican; Nat. Union = National Union*

**Books:**

Greenberg, Judith E. *Young People's Letters to the President*. Franklin Watts, 1998.

Judson, Karen. *The Presidency of the United States*. Enslow, 1996.

Krull, Kathleen. *Lives of the Presidents. Fame, Shame (and What the Neighbors Thought)*. Harcourt, 1998.

Leiner, Katherine. *First Children*. Tambourine, 1997.

Quiri, Patricia Ryon. *The Presidency*. Children's Press, 1998.

**Websites:**

The American Presidents
• Find biographies, election results, important events during each presidency, and many more links about your favorite presidents!
> **http://www.ipl.org/div/POTUS/**

The Official Guide to the White House
• Browse through the White House past and present! Peek at art, look up the presidents and their families, and learn about the history of the presidency and the White House.
> **http://www.whitehouse.gov/**

7-Hat Challenge: Master the Roles of the President
• Travel through time in this interactive quiz that outlines the many different roles presidents must play.
> **http://teacher.scholastic.com/scholasticnews/games_quizzes/president_roles**

American Presidents: Life Portraits
• C-SPAN offers detailed information about each president and offers many tips for teachers and students alike. Read letters from presidents and participate in an online student scavenger hunt!
> **http://www.americanpresidents.org/classroom**